SDMS
3-05
F01
95

ACTION SPORTS
MOTORCYCLE
GRAND PRIX RACING

Joe Herran and Ron Thomas

CHELSEA HOUSE
PUBLISHERS
A Haights Cross Communications Company
Philadelphia

This edition first published in 2003 in the United States of America by Chelsea House Publishers, a subsidiary of Haights Cross Communications.

Reprinted 2003

Chelsea House Publishers
1974 Sproul Road, Suite 400
Broomall, PA 19008-0914

The Chelsea House world wide web address is www.chelseahouse.com

Library of Congress Cataloging-in-Publication Data Applied for.
ISBN 0-7910-7001-8

First published in 2002 by
MACMILLAN EDUCATION AUSTRALIA PTY LTD
627 Chapel Street, South Yarra, Australia, 3141

Copyright © Joe Herran and Ron Thomas 2002
Copyright in photographs © individual photographers as credited
Edited by Miriana Dasovic
Text design by Karen Young
Cover design by Karen Young
Illustrations by Nives Porcellato and Andy Craig
Page layout by Raul Diche
Photo research by Legend Images

Printed in China

Acknowledgements
Cover photo: Grand Prix motorcycle riders, courtesy of Sport the library.

Australian Picture Library/Empics, pp. 20, 26 (left); Ducati, p. 21 (bottom); Ferrari, p. 14; Getty Images/Allsport, pp. 6, 11, 17, 18, 19 (top), 21 (top); Getty Images/Hulton, pp. 28 (right), 29 (left); Motorcycle Hall of Fame Museum, USA, p. 28 (left); Reuters, p. 27 (left); Sport the library, pp. 4, 5 (left), 9, 24, 25, 26 (right), 27 (right), 29 (right), 30 (top); TT Circuit Assen, p. 23; Yamaha, pp. 5 (center and right), 10, 13, 15, 30 (bottom).

While every care has been taken to trace and acknowledge copyright the publisher tenders their apologies for any accidental infringement where copyright has proved untraceable.

CONTENTS

INTRODUCTION

In this book you will read about:

• how Grand Prix motorcycles are built and tested
• how Grand Prix races are staged and judged
• the people who make up the support teams for each rider
• Grand Prix motorcycle venues
• the top riders in the sport
• the history of the sport.

In the beginning

The first motorcycles were built in Europe and the first motorcycle race also took place there. One of the earliest races was run in France in July 1894, between the cities Paris and Rouen. In 1895, motorcycle races between cities were held in both Italy and the United States. In the early 1900s, short-circuit races became popular. The competing motorcycles raced on **banked tracks**. The first international race between countries took place in France in 1904. It was called the Coupe International and was run over 17 miles (27 kilometers). Each competing country was allowed to enter three motorcycles. The race was won by a French driver named Demester at an average speed of 45 miles (72.5 kilometers) per hour.

Motorcycle Grand Prix racing today

Grand Prix motorcycle racing is a spectacular and fast-moving sport enjoyed by millions of spectators worldwide. Using the most advanced technology, teams of engineers, highly skilled riders, mechanics and designers work to build motorcycles to compete in Grand Prix events around the world.

WHAT IS GRAND PRIX MOTORCYCLE RACING?

Grand Prix motorcycle racing is organized and run by the Federation Internationale de Motocyclisme (FIM). The FIM organizes most international motorcycling events as well as all Grand Prix motorcycle racing events. It has established a sporting code of rules and regulations in each discipline of motorcycle racing, as well as technical rules to ensure that all motorcycles are safe. There is also an environmental code that sets the minimum standards for racetracks that hold motorcycle events. A drug code ensures that Grand Prix events are drug-free.

Bike classifications

Grand Prix motorcycles come in three classifications: 125 cc, 250 cc and 500 cc. These bikes are specially designed to meet the technical requirements of Grand Prix racing and are not available for sale to the public. The 500 cc class is the top classification. It contains some of the fastest and most powerful bikes. On the **straight**, 500 cc motorcycles can reach 200 miles (322 kilometers) per hour. These bikes are difficult to ride, so only a small number of highly skilled people can ride them.

Grand Prix motorcycle racing events are held on specially built **circuits**. Such circuits are also used for other motor sports, including Formula One motor car racing. All three classifications have their final race on the day of the Grand Prix. Races for the 125 cc bikes are held first, followed by the 250 cc bikes and finishing with the 500 cc bikes.

125 CC

250 CC

500 CC

MOTORCYCLE RACING
GEAR

The Grand Prix motorcycle

There are major differences between motorcycles, and the way they are constructed depends on how they will be used. A Grand Prix motorcycle is built for use only on the racetrack.

The engine

The engine is the mechanism that makes the motorcycle run. The engine takes in fuel and burns it to create the energy that drives the **pistons**. Most Grand Prix bikes use a powerful, two-stroke engine.

Frames and suspension

A Grand Prix motorcycle has an **aerodynamic** design and a lightweight, very rigid frame. These features help the bike to reach high speeds and to turn sharp corners quickly and safely.

The front and back of the motorcycle have a suspension system. The suspension helps absorb any bumps the rider may encounter, and helps the rider withstand the forces generated during high-speed turns.

Wheel
Frame
Engine
Tire
Brakes
Suspension

Wheels, tires and brakes

Wheels are made of aluminum or **magnesium** for strength. Tires are fat and **slick**. Usually the rear tire is a little wider than the front tire, to help the rider make sharp turns at high speeds. The disc brake system has a single steel disc, which is gripped by twin brake pads.

Designing the Grand Prix motorcycle

Grand Prix motorcycles are constructed by engineers, mechanics and designers with help from the riders. These people are known as the team. Designers first build a **simulation** of the bike and test it on a computer. The performance of a Grand Prix motorcycle depends on the power of the motor and the weight and shape of the bike's body. Grand Prix motorcycles have a motor specially designed for great power and speed. Their engines are very heavy, so the designers try to avoid adding to the weight by making the frames from light and strong materials. The motorcycle is also designed to be as **streamlined** as possible. This allows it to attain great speeds and make the many turns found on a Grand Prix circuit.

1. Fuel is sucked in as the piston moves up the cylinder

— Piston
— Cylinder
— Inlet port

2. The spark plug ignites the fuel, forcing the piston down the cylinder

— Spark plug
Power stroke
— Connecting rod

3. As burnt gases leave the exhaust, fresh fuel flows in above the piston

Outlet port
Crank shaft

4. The piston moves up ready for the next power stroke

TWO-STROKE ENGINE

Testing the Grand Prix motorcycle

Once the first phase of the design has been completed, a test bike is built for the engineers to work on. This bike is first tested in a wind tunnel to check that the air flows smoothly around the bike. Changes can then be made to improve the design and make the bike faster. The bike is then tested for safety in crash tests.

After hundreds of hours of work, the motorcycle is completed and ready for testing on the track before the start of the Grand Prix season. Once the team is happy with the bike, it is painted in the team colors and is ready for competition. Two bikes are built for each Grand Prix event.

ACTION FACT

When designing a Grand Prix motorcycle, the designers take into account the size of the rider. This is necessary because the shape of the rider on the bike affects how streamlined the bike will be.

The motorcycle rider's gear

Helmet

The helmet protects the rider's head in a fall. It is also designed to reduce the effect of wind and noise on the rider. Built-in ventilation ducts keep the head cool.

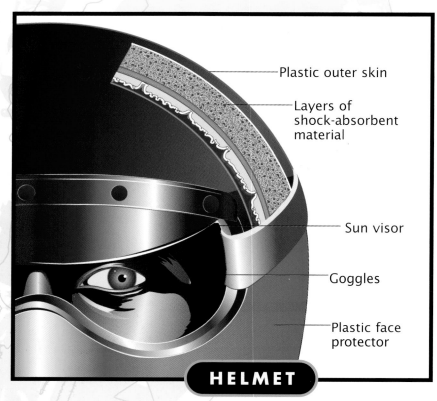

- Plastic outer skin
- Layers of shock-absorbent material
- Sun visor
- Goggles
- Plastic face protector

HELMET

Visor

The visor, through which the rider sees, must be tough enough to withstand being hit by the stones that are thrown up from the track. The visor has several see-through adhesive strips on it. When the top strip becomes dirty, the rider simply peels it off.

Leather suit

The rider's suit is made of kangaroo skin, which is the toughest and lightest leather available. Extra protection is provided by the carbon fiber and **Kevlar** inserts on the spine, shoulders, chest and limbs. This tough leather suit is sometimes referred to as body armor.

Gloves

Gloves are designed to allow the rider's hands and wrists to move freely. There are carbon fiber inserts on the knuckles and Kevlar padding for protection.

Knee pads

When turning a corner of the track, the rider leans so far out that the knee pads touch the ground. The pads help the rider to stay balanced during the turn while protecting the knees.

Boots

A carbon fiber inner-shell and a leather outer layer reinforce the ankle and toes. These minimize injury in a fall.

Mouth guard

Many Grand Prix motorcycle riders use mouth guards to protect the teeth and mouth in case of accidents.

Helmet

Visor

Mouth guard

Leather suit

Gloves

Knee pads

Boots

SKILLS, TRICKS AND
TECHNIQUES

Riding a motorcycle

Balancing on the moving bike is one of the first skills that must be mastered when learning to ride a motorcycle. When traveling in a straight line, riders must keep their weight equally balanced on both sides of the motorcycle. When turning a corner, riders must make sure not to overbalance or they will fall off.

The right hand controls the twist-grip throttle with the fingers reaching forward to pull on the front brake lever

The fingers of the left hand operate the clutch lever, pulling it in every time the gears are changed

The right foot presses down to work the rear brake lever

The left foot operates the gear-shift lever

GRAND PRIX RACING:
THE RULES

All Grand Prix events must follow the procedures set out by the FIM. The federation has the right to inspect any track, and the track must comply with all the FIM standards. Before the racing starts, the race director, along with the referee and the clerk of the course, carry out a track inspection.

Here are some of the FIM racing rules:

- Only pure methanol may be used in the bikes.
- Each rider is allowed a maximum of two motorcycles in the pits on race day.
- All bikes must have a rear wheel dirt deflector.
- Only licensed riders are allowed to compete in Grand Prix events.
- The motorcycle must clearly display the rider's number. The helmet must also have the number clearly printed on it on the right-hand side above the goggle strap.
- Only team members are allowed in the pits during the race, and they must all be dressed in team colors.

All motorcycles competing in any Grand Prix event must be Grand Prix-kitted:

↗ Race officials check each motorcycle to make sure that it complies with the racing rules.

- They cannot have any lights, starting mechanisms, street equipment or associated brackets.
- They must have low, narrow handlebars (maximum width of $31\frac{1}{2}$ inches (80 centimeters)) and **fairings** are encouraged.
- They must be equipped with racing exhaust systems.
- Front disc brakes are prohibited. Rear disc brakes are permitted.
- Magnesium engine cases are allowed in the 500 cc class.
- The rims on the bikes must be at least $17\frac{3}{4}$ inches (45 centimeters) in diameter.

THE GRAND PRIX RACING
TEAM

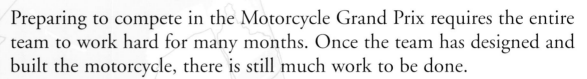

Preparing to compete in the Motorcycle Grand Prix requires the entire team to work hard for many months. Once the team has designed and built the motorcycle, there is still much work to be done.

In the pits, all team members must wear the team colors. The name of the team rider as well as the team member's job must be shown on the back of each uniform.

Members of the team

Rider

The rider is a key member of the team, and the one that is most visible. Riders must use all their skills to get the best out of their machines. Grand Prix motorcycle riders are specially trained and highly skilled.

Team manager

The team manager is in charge of the team and makes all the decisions about the work of the team.

Software engineer

The software engineer is in charge of all electronics used on the bike. The software engineer also gathers and sorts data received by computers during practice and race sessions, and distributes it to other team members. This helps others in the team adjust the motor or other parts of the motorcycle to gain more speed and power.

Technical adviser

The technical adviser is the problem-solver of the team. Any difficulties that the team may encounter with the bike are analyzed by the technical adviser, who looks for and applies engineering solutions. The technical adviser's recommendations are passed on to the mechanics in the garage.

A large number of people make up a Grand Prix racing team.

Chief mechanic

The chief mechanic is responsible for setting up the bike to achieve the best possible result over a Grand Prix weekend. The chief mechanic is also in charge of the development of the motorcycle and oversees the other mechanics on the team.

Mechanics

Mechanics work under instruction from the chief mechanic. Their job is to prepare the bike so that it gives maximum performance during the race.

Brake, suspension and tire specialists

These specialists fit the equipment to the bike that best suits the conditions of the circuit on race day.

Parts and logistics specialists

These specialists make sure that all equipment is checked and replaced if necessary so that nothing fails during a race.

Personal or physical therapist

The rider's therapist plans a program of exercise and a diet to help keep the rider in top shape during the season. If the rider is injured, the therapist will help the rider recover as quickly as possible.

Caterers

Full-time chefs travel with the team, preparing food for the whole team. The rider in particular must be well fed and kept healthy.

RIDER
FITNESS

Riders in Grand Prix 500 cc competitions must be physically fit. The **acceleration** and sharp turns in 500 cc racing place great strain on a rider's body. The rider is buffeted around the bends and extreme corners of the track, so neck and back muscles must be strong to cope with the forces placed on them. During the race, a rider loses body fluids rapidly. This can lead to **dehydration**, muscle cramps and a loss of concentration. These are dangerous conditions for a rider in control of a machine traveling at more than 186 miles (300 kilometers) per hour.

Riders often crash and fall off their bikes. To avoid serious injury, they must be fit and know how to fall off their bikes when they lose their balance. The proper way of falling off is to relax the body and not tense up during the fall. This method makes it less likely that the fall will break bones or cause other serious injuries.

A physical therapist is part of the race team. The physical therapist plans a program of exercises for the rider that build stamina, strength and concentration. The therapist supervises what the rider eats and makes sure that the diet is helping to keep the rider fit. If a rider is injured, the physical therapist will work with the rider to help make the recovery as quick as possible.

↗ Riders keep fit by jogging, cycling or working out in a gym.

PRACTICING FOR THE
GRAND PRIX

During a Grand Prix meeting, a number of practice sessions are held on the days before the race. Each of the Grand Prix circuits has a different number of turns and is shaped differently. It is important that the rider knows the circuit very well before racing on it.

Before a practice ride, a safety check on the engine and on every other part of the bike is carried out by the mechanics. The bike is also inspected to make sure it has been built to the current standards of the FIM. This includes weighing the bike. According to the FIM rules, there can be no practice on race day.

The practice sessions are important for all members of the racing team. Much computer data is compiled by the team members to check how the motorcycle and rider are performing. This helps the team work on the motorcycle to get the fastest times out of the machine. Race tactics are discussed with the team after these sessions.

Time trials are held before the day of the Grand Prix. Riders' times are recorded during the official practice runs, and the results determine where on the **grid** a rider will be placed for the Grand Prix race. The rider with the fastest time will start on the **pole position**.

↗ Practice sessions give the rider a feel for the track before the big race.

SAFETY AT THE TRACK

It is the job of the officials at each Grand Prix race to make sure that the track surface has been prepared properly. A poor track could cause serious injury to the riders.

> ◤ The track must be graded after each race or it wears down and becomes dangerous to drive on.

How a racing track deteriorates after each race

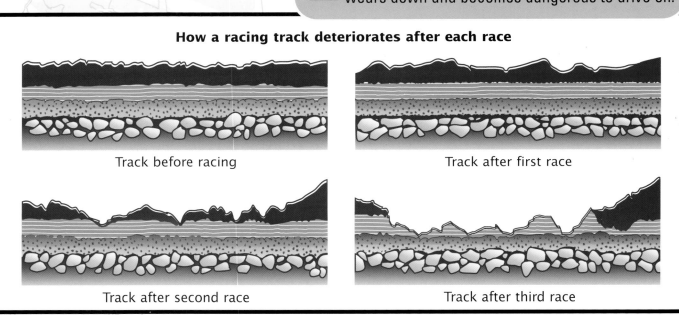

Track before racing

Track after first race

Track after second race

Track after third race

Flags and lights

When the riders line up for the start of the race, a red light glows on the official board until all the riders have taken their places on the grid. When the red light goes out, the race begins.

A green flag or green lights indicate that the course is clear of hazards.

A yellow-and-red striped flag warns of oil, water or another substance on the track. Riders must take care.

A blue flag warns that a slower rider is about to be overtaken by a faster rider. (Slower riders are not allowed to block or slow down faster riders.)

When the flag is held still, the faster rider is approaching the slower rider. When the flag is being waved, the faster rider is about to overtake.

A yellow flag or yellow flashing lights warn of danger on a section of the track. Riders are not allowed to pass one another while the yellow flag or yellow lights are displayed.

A white flag warns of a slow-moving car, ambulance or similar vehicle on the track. When the flag is held still, the rider can expect to encounter the vehicle soon. When the flag is being waved, it indicates that the vehicle is already on the rider's section of the track. Riders are not allowed to pass one another while a white flag is displayed.

A black flag and an orange disc with a rider's number on it indicate that the rider must stop at the pits at the end of the current **lap**.

A red flag or red light indicates that the practice session or race has been interrupted, and all riders must leave the track slowly and return to the pits.

The black-and-white checkered flag signals the finish of the race or practice session.

Drug code

All competitors are required to follow the strict anti-doping regulations overseen by the FIM. Riders are allowed to take certain medicines to help with the treatment of conditions such as asthma, colds, coughs and the flu. Riders can be tested at any time during, before or after a competition.

↗ The race ends at the checkered flag.

OFFICIALS AT THE
GRAND PRIX

The officials on the Grand Prix circuit have the responsibility of making sure that the race is safe for both spectators and riders. All motorcycles are checked carefully by both the rider's team and the course officials before the start of the race. At any time during the race, a rider may be asked by an official to leave the track if the official decides that a motorcycle is unsafe. The officials give recognized signals to the riders by means of flags, boards or lights.

Referee

The referee is in charge of the event and is responsible for ensuring that all rules and regulations are observed.

Clerk of the course

This official ensures that the track has been prepared properly before the practice sessions begin. The clerk of the course reports to the referee, and has control over all other officials except the referee.

Technical steward

The technical steward checks that all machines meet the technical requirements of the FIM.

↗ An official holds up a sign to indicate to the riders when the race will start.

Timekeeper

The timekeeper is responsible for the timing of all heats in the event.

Doctor

A doctor is on duty to take care of any medical needs or emergencies.

Announcer

The announcer must give the public the results of each heat and information about who is racing.

Pits' marshal

The pits' marshal makes sure that only riders and their mechanics are in the pits, and that all emergency equipment is in order. The pit marshal also ensures that all bikes have correct numbers and riders are wearing correct helmet colors.

Starting marshal

The starting marshal makes sure that the riders are in their proper positions at the start of each race. The starting marshal also ensures that the flag signals used to show the riders that the last lap is coming are displayed at the appropriate time.

Flag marshals

There are flag marshals at each bend in the course. They display flags after receiving information from the referee or from the starting marshal.

Flag marshals at work. The yellow-and-red striped flag is used to warn drivers of oil or water on the track.

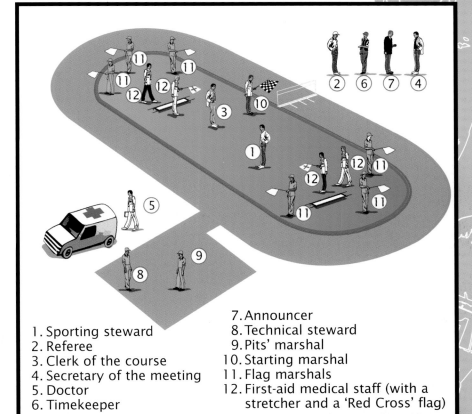

1. Sporting steward
2. Referee
3. Clerk of the course
4. Secretary of the meeting
5. Doctor
6. Timekeeper
7. Announcer
8. Technical steward
9. Pits' marshal
10. Starting marshal
11. Flag marshals
12. First-aid medical staff (with a stretcher and a 'Red Cross' flag)

RACING OFFICIALS AT THE TRACK

IN COMPETITION

The three races

Three races are run on Grand Prix race day. The first is the 125 cc race. This ranges from 17 to 26 laps, depending on the length of the track. The 250 cc is the second race, which is 18 to 27 laps. The final race of the day is the 500 cc race, which is 20 to 30 laps.

↘ **ACTION FACT**

Because each Grand Prix circuit is a different length, Grand Prix races do not have the same number of laps per race.

Grid positions

Before each event begins, the riders line up in their grid positions. The rider who scored the fastest time in the practice runs has the pole position, the second-fastest rider is in the number two position and so on. Before the race begins, there is a warm-up lap of the field. This gives the riders a chance to warm up their brakes and their tires. Then the riders again line up in their grid positions for the start of the race.

The starting marshal then checks that all riders are in their correct places on the grid. The riders wait for the red light on the official board to go out. This signals the beginning of the race.

↗ Riders line up on the grid before the race begins.

Strategy and balance

During the race, riders must use **strategy** to get in the best possible position. Not every rider wants to reach first place from the start of the race. Often riders find it easier to sit in second or third place during most of the race, and pass other riders only toward the end of the race.

This strategy also allows them to see what the riders ahead of them are doing.

It is difficult to pass another motorcycle during a race, so a rider must time the pass carefully to avoid falling off the bike. A trick used by good riders is called slipstreaming. This occurs when one rider follows another rider very closely, sheltering from the oncoming wind. The second rider thus avoids being slowed down by air resistance or drag.

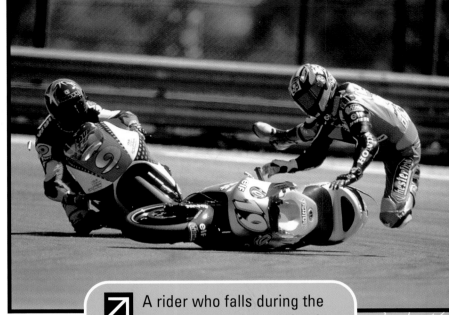

↗ A rider who falls during the race is allowed to get back on the bike and continue in the race if the motorcycle is undamaged.

After the race

The podium ceremony

Standing on the **podium**, the riders receive their prizes while the national anthem of the winner's country is played. The teams of these three riders are also awarded prizes.

The World Champion rider

Grand Prix points are awarded to the winner and their team. The winner of the Grand Prix is awarded 25 points, the second place-winner gets 20 points, third place gets 16 points and fourth place gets 13 points. At the end of the season, the points are added to reveal the World Champion rider.

ACTION FACT

It is possible to win the Grand Prix World Championship without winning a race. This happens because points are awarded to the rider's team. At the end of the season, the team with the most points wins the Constructor's Cup as the champion team.

↘ The riders who finish the race in first, second and third positions attend the prize-giving ceremony on the podium after the race.

Motorcycle Grand Prix circuits

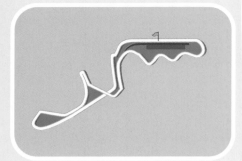

Grand Prix of Japan

Suzuka, Japan

- Track is 5.859 kilometers long.
- In 1963, this was the venue for the first world championship motorcycle event to be held in Japan. This track is also used for Formula One motorcar racing, the eight-hour endurance World Championship and many other motor sports.

Gauloises Africa's Grand Prix

Phakisa Freeway, South Africa

- Track is 4.242 kilometers long.
- Built in the desert in South Africa, this is one of the newest race circuits on the **MotoGP** itinerary.

Gran Premio Marlboro De Espana

Jerez, Spain

- Track is 4.423 kilometers long.

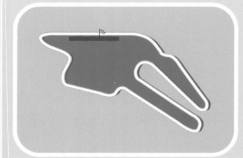

Grand Prix of France

Le Mans, France

- Track is 4.305 kilometers long.
- Part of the track, called the Bugatti Circuit, is also home to the Le Mans 24-hour race and is the venue for touring car races and a Formula One Grand Prix race every year.

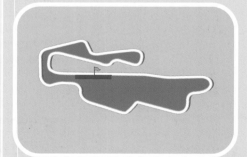

Gran Premio Cinzano D'Italia

Mugello, Italy

- Track is 5.245 kilometers long.
- This circuit is considered to be one of the safest racetracks in the world.

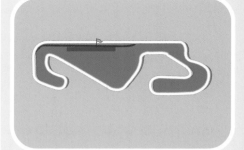

Gran Premi Marlboro de Catalunya

Circuit de Catalunya, Spain

- Track is 4.727 kilometers long.
- Circuit de Catalunya is considered to be one of the best-designed racetracks in the world.

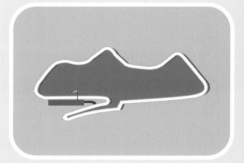

Cinzano British Grand Prix

Donington Park, Great Britain

- Track is 4.023 kilometers long.

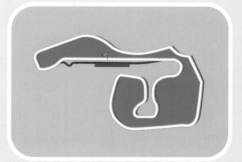

Cinzano Motorrad Grand Prix Deutschland

Sachsenring Circuit, Germany

- Track is 3.508 kilometers long.
- This circuit is used as a rider training center.

Gauloises Ceske Republiky Grand Prix

Autodrom Brno, Czech Republic

- Track is 5.403 kilometers long.

Pacific Grand Prix of Motegi

Motegi, Japan

- Track is 4.801 kilometers long.

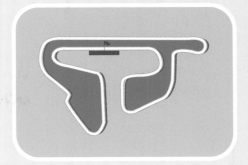

Cinzano Rio Grand Prix

Nelson Piquet, Brazil

- Track is 4.933 kilometers long.

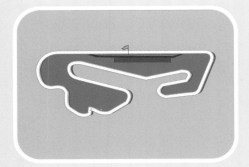

Grande Premo Marlboro De Portugal

Estoril, Portugal

- Track is 4.182 kilometers long.

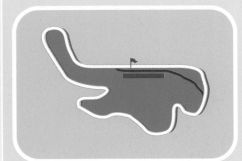

Qantas Australian Grand Prix

Phillip Island, Australia

- Track is 4.448 kilometers long.
- Motor car racing began at Phillip Island in the 1920s and the first motorcycle race took place there in 1931.

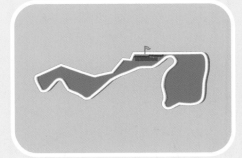

Rizla Dutch TT, Circuit van Drenthe

Assen, Netherlands

- Track is 6.049 kilometers long.
- Circuit van Drenthe is the longest course in Grand Prix motorcycle racing.

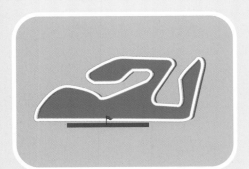

Gran Premio Marlboro De La Comunitat Valenciana

Comunitat Valenciana, Spain

- Track is 4.005 kilometers long.

Malaysian Motorcycle Grand Prix

Sepang Circuit, Malaysia

- Track is 5.548 kilometers long.

CIRCUIT VAN DRENTHE

GRAND PRIX
CHAMPIONS

Many of the top motorcycle riders started out riding less-powerful bikes before graduating to bigger motorcycles such as the 500 cc Grand Prix bikes. Grand Prix motorcycle champions come from many countries including the United States, Japan, Australia, Italy and Brazil. The first female rider, Katja Poensgen from Germany, competed in the Grand Prix 250 cc class in 2001.

↗ Kenny Roberts Jr.

- Nationality: American
- Born: July 25, 1973
- Team: Telefonica Movistar Suzuki
- Bike: Suzuki Class 500 cc
- Kenny is the son of a three-time world champion, Kenny Roberts Sr. Kenny learned to ride bikes on dirt tracks and competed in 250 cc Grand Prix racing before he took up 500 cc racing.

Statistics

- World Champion in 500 cc racing in 2000
- Has competed in 73 500 cc races
- 8 x 1st place wins
- 6 x 2nd place wins
- 3 x 3rd place wins

↗ Garry McCoy

- Nationality: Australian
- Born: April 18, 1972
- Team: Red Bull Yamaha WCM
- Bike: Yamaha Class 500 cc
- Competed in 125 cc Grand Prix racing before he started racing in the 500 cc class

Statistics

- Placed sixth in the World 500 cc Championship in 2000
- Has competed in 36 500 cc races
- 3 x 1st place wins
- 7 x 2nd place wins
- 4 x 3rd place wins

↗ Norick Abe

- Nationality: Japanese
- Born: September 7, 1975
- Team: Antena 3 Yamaha-d'Antin
- Bike: Yamaha Class 500 cc
- Unlike many other riders, Norick did not compete in other classes of less-powerful Grand Prix bikes before starting to ride 500 cc bikes.

Statistics

- In 1996, won the Suzuka Grand Prix and became the first Japanese rider to win a Japanese Grand Prix 500 cc event
- Finished seventh in the World Championships in 2000
- Has competed in 92 500 cc races
- 3 x 1st place wins
- 3 x 2nd place wins
- 10 x 3rd place wins

↗ Valentino Rossi

- Nationality: Italian
- Born: February 16, 1979
- Team: Nastro Azzurro Honda
- Bike: Honda Class 500 cc
- Before racing in the 500 cc class, Valentino raced in the 125 cc and 250 cc classes. Valentino's father, Grazziano, was a famous Grand Prix rider in the 1970s.

Statistics

- Valentino had been riding for just one year when he came second in the World Championships in 2000.
- Has competed in sixteen 500 cc races
- 2 x 1st place wins
- 3 x 2nd place wins
- 5 x 3rd place wins

↗ Alex Barros

- Nationality: Brazilian
- Born: October 18, 1970
- Team: West Honda Pons
- Bike: Honda Class 500 cc
- Alex is the most experienced rider in the circuit today. He competed in the 125 cc and 250 cc classes in Grand Prix racing before moving to 500 cc.
- He made his Grand Prix debut in 1988 at the age of 15.

Statistics

- The only rider to have won both the 125 cc and 250 cc Brazilian Grand Prix
- Finished fourth in the World Championships in 2000
- Has competed in 147 500 cc races
- 3 x 1st place wins
- 6 x 2nd place wins
- 5 x 3rd place wins

↗ Katja Poensgen

- Nationality: German
- Born: September 23, 1976
- Team: Umoto
- Bike: Aprilia Class 250 cc
- Katja became the first female motorcycle rider to compete in Grand Prix motorcycle racing when she rode in the 250 cc Grand Prix in 2001.
- Katja's father was a former **motocross** and **enduro** rider. At four years of age, she attended races with her father. By the age of nine she had decided that she wanted to race motorcycles. At first her parents were not keen on the idea, but Katja got her first motorbike when she turned 14. She began competing, and at 17 years of age was the first female to win the Junior Cup in Germany. By the time she was 18, she was competing in the 125 cc German competition.

↗ Max Biaggi

- Nationality: Italian
- Born: June 26, 1971
- Team: Marlboro Yamaha
- Bike: Yamaha Class 500 cc
- Max was born in Rome. He was soccer-crazy, and he wanted to play soccer for the AS Roma soccer team. In 1988 he went with a friend to a local motorcycle track and found that he loved riding motorbikes. Max started racing professionally in 1989, with his father as his mechanic.

Statistics

- Won the 1991 250 cc European Championship and became a Grand Prix rider in 1992
- Won the 250 cc Grand Prix World Championship 1994–1997
- In 1998, he changed to 500 cc Grand Prix racing and was the first rookie in 25 years to win his first 500 cc race in Japan
- In 1998, finished second in the 500 cc Grand Prix World Championships
- In 2000, finished third in the 500 cc Grand Prix World Championships
- Has won four world championships
- Recorded 33 pole positions
- Won 23 Grand Prix races

1885	1892	1894	1895	1904	1907	1930s
Gottlieb Daimler built the first motorcycle. The bike had smaller outrigger wheels on each side and was made of wood.	The first two-wheeler motorbike was invented, called the Millet. It had an engine in the hub of its rear wheel.	The first major motorbike event was held in France, on the roads between the cities of Paris and Rouen.	The French firm of DeDion-Buton built an engine that was small, light and easy to manufacture. It was the engine used in many early motorbikes. The first motorbike races were held in Italy and the United States.	The first international race, the Coupe International, was held in France. A French rider, Demester, won at an average speed of 45 miles (72.5 kilometers) per hour. The Federation Internationale des Clubs Motorcyclists was formed to regulate motorcycle races throughout Europe.	The first race circuit was built in Brooklands, Britain. The circuit was egg-shaped and 2.8 miles (4.5 kilometers) long.	There was great competition between different motorcycle manufacturers in Germany, Italy and Britain as each tried to build the fastest motorcycle and win in the various races held throughout Europe.

1885

1892

1907

1939	1949	1970s	1978–1980	1990s	2000	2002
All motorcycle racing ended when World War II started. Motorcycles were used as army vehicles during the war.	The first Grand Prix season after the war was held. The Grand Prix competition included 125 cc, 250 cc, 350 cc, 500 cc and sidecars.	The two-stroke engine for 500 cc motorcycles was introduced by Yamaha.	Kenny Roberts of the United States won the 500 cc championship three years in a row.	Grand Prix competitions were held around the world.

Grand Prix motorcycle racing was limited to three classes: 125 cc, 250 cc and 500 cc. | Kenny Roberts Jr. won the 500 cc championship. This was the first time that a former champion's son had won the title. | The Grand Prix season adds the 990 cc four-stroke bikes, which are more powerful than the 500 cc bikes. |

1939

2000

RELATED ACTION SPORTS

Motocross

Motocross bikes are specially made to be ridden at high speed on rough dirt and mud tracks. The bikes are strong, lightweight and very tall, so that the engine and frame do not hit the ground while traveling over rough surfaces. The seat is about 3 feet (1 meter) from the ground.

The tracks have difficult obstacles, as well as steep hills that the riders take at high speeds before leaping off and landing far down on the other side. Sometimes motocross tracks are built in big indoor arenas. Motocross was once called 'scrambling'.

MOTOCROSS

Superbikes

Superbikes are the most powerful racing motorcycles. Superbikes look like Grand Prix racing bikes, but are made to be ridden on the road and not the track. Some superbikes can travel at speeds of up to 190 miles (306 kilometers) per hour, and are specially designed to turn corners at these high speeds. The rider sits very low, or may even lie almost flat on the stomach with arms stretched in front and feet behind. Some superbikes can accelerate from 0 to 60 miles (100 kilometers) per hour in about three seconds.

World Superbike racing has become very popular since it began in 1988. There are two basic types of superbikes in competition: those with 750 cc four-cylinder engines, and the twin-cylinder 1000 cc machines.

SUPERBIKES

GLOSSARY

acceleration increase in speed

aerodynamic the qualities of a motorcycle that affect the way it moves through air, particularly what makes it travel faster

banked tracks artificial slopes built beside a racing track so that the motorcycles can be ridden at high speed around bends

circuit another name for the racetrack

dehydration extreme loss of bodily fluids

enduro a type of motorcycle endurance racing

fairing the outer covering of a motorcycle. The fairing covers the engine and other workings of the motorcycle. This makes the bike more streamlined

grid area on the track where the motorcycles line up for the start of the race

Kevlar an artificial material that is extremely strong and heat-resistant

lap a single round of the racing track

magnesium a light metal alloy used in the manufacture of motorcycles

motocross a type of motorcycle racing in which bikes are ridden at high speeds on rough dirt and mud tracks

MotoGP a type of motorcycle racing

piston a moveable cylinder inside an engine

podium the place where awards are made after the race

pole position the first position in the starting grid, slightly ahead of the others

simulation a computer image of a new design that shows what the motorcycle will be like when it is built

slick refers to tires that are smooth and have little or no tread

straight the part of a race circuit track without curves

strategy planning how a race will be run

streamlined shaped so that the motorbike moves with little wind resistance

INDEX